SLEEPING WITH THE ENEMY

An Unconscious Fellowship with Spirit Beings

FRANK H. YOUNG

Let not the sun go down on your wrath.
[Ephesians 4:26]

WESTBOW°
PRESS
A DIVISION OF THOMAS NELSON
& ZONDERVAN

WestBow Press books may be ordered through
booksellers or by contacting:

WestBow Press
A Division of Thomas Nelson
1663 Liberty Drive
Bloomington, IN 47403
www.westbowpress.com
1 (866) 928-1240

Because of the dynamic nature of the Internet, any web addresses or
links contained in this book may have changed since publication and
may no longer be valid. The views expressed in this work are solely those
of the author and do not necessarily reflect the views of the publisher,
and the publisher hereby disclaims any responsibility for them.

Any people depicted in stock imagery provided by Thinkstock are models,
and such images are being used for illustrative purposes only.
Certain stock imagery © Thinkstock.

ISBN: 978-1-4908-2178-8 (sc)
ISBN: 978-1-4908-2179-5 (e)

Library of Congress Control Number: 2014900663

Printed in the United States of America.

WestBow Press rev. date: 01/09/2014

CONTENTS

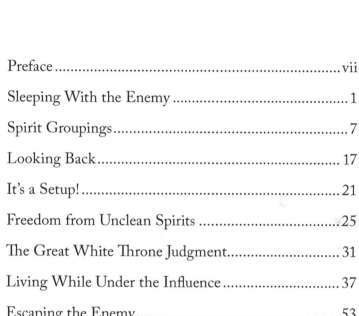

PREFACE

I thank God for my wife, Barbara, whom He chose to be a leading role in His plan to deliver me from many unclean spirits which had invaded my life at a very young age.

We all have had ungodly, unclean, unrighteous spirits to invade us. Some of them may be present before we are born; others invade us as young children, teens, etc.

There are two kinds of spirits in existence: (1) the Holy Spirit, which is of God and (2) the nearly countless spirits of the devil, [Satan].

God is one spirit. The Holy Spirit is the Spirit of God which co-exist with God, the Father, and God, the Son. God is the self-existing Creator of all things, but Satan is a created being.

God is omnipresent, [everywhere present at the same time]. Satan cannot be so. Because he was created and does not co-exist with God, Satan has to have an agency of many spirits working in many places so that his presence might be variable.

In his own confession, Satan said, "I will ascend into heaven, I will exalt my throne above the stars of God: I will sit also upon the mount of the congregation, in the sides of the north: I will ascend above the heights of the clouds: I will be "like" the most high." (Isaiah 14:13,14)

There is only one Holy Spirit, [Spirit of God]. All other spirits, whether called unclean, demonic, or fallen angels, are of the devil. These satanic, unclean, ungodly spirits are enemies of both God and man. And when we allow them to constantly indwell us, we are--in a spiritual sense--sleeping with the enemy.

Ephesians 6:12 [KJV] says, "For we wrestle not against flesh and blood, but against principalities, against powers, against the rulers of the <u>darkness</u> of this world, against spiritual wickedness in high places".

Eph. 6:11 says, "Put on the whole armor of God, that ye may be able to stand against the wiles of the devil".

The above Scriptures describe what is called by many Bible scholars, '<u>spiritual warfare</u>'. The battle is spiritual. The arena is spiritual. The weapons are spiritual, and the warriors are spiritual, born-again, and godly people, warring against spirit beings.

Though the believer is not noted to become possessed by unclean or demonic spirits, yet no one is exempt of being subject to occupying or harboring these unwanted entities.

How they enter, how they stay and why, and how to clean the house is further described in this book.

Since spirits don't die or sleep, we sleep with them (after they enter into us) because they are still with us as we sleep.

Read this book and let's do something about it by using the weapons that God has given us to rule as citizens in the Kingdom of God.

Let us stop the enemy in his tracks as he and his countless agents seek to oppose all that God has in store for His children to have, do and be.

SLEEPING WITH THE ENEMY

A catchy phrase like "sleeping with the enemy" may send the mind of many into thinking of husbands and wives being enemies of one another, yet sleeping together. Even if this is true in some cases, most of them would never be enemies to one another if they knew who the real enemy was: _the invisible entity that seems to throw bricks, then hide his hand._

The idea of this book is to expose such invisible entities, or spiritual influences that are working behind the scenes in the life of every human being. The Bible calls them principalities, powers, rulers of the darkness of this world and spiritual wickedness in high places. (Eph. 6:12)

These enemies aren't new. They manifested in heaven before the creation of man. (Is. 14:12) One of the schemes in their activities is to lie on God, (Gen. 3:4) and bring shame on man (Gen. 3:10).

*Man was still in the infancy of his creative being when he was tricked into fearing his best friend, [God], his

creator, and to blame others for his mistakes (as in Adam's phrase, "the woman that you gave me"].

Similarly, are we in the infancy of our natural lives when we are babies--even as unborn babies and children--when unclean spirits invade our being. As if the spirit of fear doesn't come soon enough, we are taught to fear. Firstly, we are taught to fear our parents, when they dare us to do certain things with the threat of spanking us for doing them. We teach ourselves to lie, either for fear of getting a whipping, or the fear of being told no we can't do this, or can't have that, etc. Not realizing that fear is a spirit, lying is a spirit, and neither of them are of God.

Just as Adam and Eve were open to unwanted entities in their infancy as created beings, so are we opened to the same type of spirits in the infancy of our childhood. By the time many of us become adults, we may be loaded with a variety of ungodly invaders which seek to acquire physical bodies in order that Satan may carry out his plan to imitate God. (Mt. 12: 43-45)

In the Old Testament, the people of God may have had spiritual opposition, but not spiritual warfare, probably because they had no spiritual weapons. Therefore, God divinely fought spiritual battles in their behalf, as in 2 Kings 19:35.

Since the day of Pentecost, born-again believers, [New Testament saints] have been equipped with spiritual weapons in order to enter into spiritual warfare. (2 Cor. 10: 3-5; Eph. 6:10-17) We have the Holy Spirit indwelling us, we have the word of God, and we have the name

Jesus and faith, as well as ministering spirits [holy angels]. (Hebrews 1:14) All of such are spiritual weapons for our warfare.

God has made us such a great part of His plan, His kingdom and purpose, that we are laborers together with him. (1 Cor. 3:9) "Therefore, my beloved brethren, be steadfast, unmovable, always abounding in the work of the Lord, for as much as you know that your labor is not in vain in the Lord. (1 Cor. 15:58) KJV

The enemy is not physical; the battle is not physical: "…for we wrestle not against flesh and blood, but against principalities, against powers, against the rulers of the *darkness* of this world, against *spiritual wickedness* in high places]. (Ephesians 6:12)

There we have it. The real battle is in the realm of the spirit. Adam and Eve didn't know that so Adam blamed Eve, and Eve blamed the serpent. Some things they could not see with their physical eyes. The invisible entity worked behind the scenes, influencing those precious creatures of God. (Gen. 3:12,13) <u>NO PROBLEM</u>! *If we obey God…* But do we really believe His word?

"And these signs shall follow them that believe; in My name they shall cast out devils; they shall speak with new tongues; they shall take up serpents; and if they drink any deadly thing, it shall not hurt them; they shall lay hands on the sick, and they shall recover. (Mk. 16: 17,18)

Do we believe that? Do we practice His word? I don't practice picking up snakes, but I do claim the faith to do whatever the Bible says I can do, as I am led by the Holy Spirit. It is being led by the Spirit of God that proves I am a son of God. (Rom. 8:14) *Keep the faith, and keep it simple.*

Frank H. Young

*Who was the very first enemy? Revelation 12:9 says, "And the great dragon was cast out, that old serpent, called the Devil and Satan, which deceived the whole world: he was cast out into the earth, and his angels were cast out with him".

*The last enemy also: "and death and hell were cast into the lake of fire, this is the second death." (Revelation 20:14)

Satan has angels, (Rev. 12:14). His angels are demons, [unclean spirits]. He needs many of them because unlike God, Satan is not omnipresent. Therefore, he, [Satan] has countless agents, [demons] working in his kingdom.

"And his tail drew the third part of the stars of heaven, and did cast them to the earth." (Revelation 12:4) Satan has been defeated every since Jesus died and rose again. But Satan's work is to keep us from knowing that we have the victory in Jesus. Therefore, if we don't know it, we cannot act on it, as we continue to go to bed each night and <u>sleep</u> with the enemy. Come out, and be free! Only Jesus can make us free!

Wherever Satan goes will eventually become chaos. Isaiah 14:17 says, "that [he] made the world as a wilderness, and destroyed the cities thereof, that opened <u>not</u> the house of his prisoners".

Without Satan and satanic beings, there would be no sin. Without sin there would be no law. Without law there would be no boundaries.

In the Garden of Eden, Satan played upon man's second most important gift, <u>imagination</u>. The first gift was the breath of God.

Regardless of God's original instructions to man, man hearing another's voice concerning the forbidden fruit would and did stir his imagination.

Yielding to his own imagination caused man to disobey God and fall from the original state of grace--to lose the original God-given kingdom. After this, God called man's imagination, vain. (Genesis 6:5).

Today, we have been given instructions concerning our imagination:

> Casting down imaginations, and every high thing that exalts itself against the knowledge of God, and bringing into captivity every thought to the obedience of Christ. (2 Cor. 10:5)

We can't escape the voices heard by Adam and Eve; we can't escape the sight of tempting things. But we don't have to yield to the pride of life as did the first man, Adam.

SPIRIT GROUPINGS

Jesus mentioned 'spirit grouping' while speaking to an audience, according to Matthew 12: 43-46.

Jesus indicated, when an unclean spirit goes out of a man, he goes into dry places seeking rest. But without a physical body, the spirit finds no rest. When he returns to the body which he left, finding his previous place still empty, he brings with him a group of kindred spirits for security and more power.

Some call kindred spirits 'familiar spirits', but I believe there is a difference.

Familiar spirits has to do with a variety of demonic activities such as, divining, sorcery, witchcraft, etc..., while kindred spirits are a family or group of spirits in association or like nature.

In kindred spirit groupings, the spirit of <u>insecurity</u> may have in his group: self-pity, loneliness, inferiority, timidity, shyness, inadequacy, etc. <u>Depression's</u> kin might be despair, dejection, discouragement, defeatism, despondency, suicide, death, etc. The spirit of <u>strife</u> may be kin to or in association with contention, argument, quarreling, fighting, etc.

Thanks to Frank and Ida Mae Hammond for their much study and sharing from their book, "Pigs in the Parlor".

Anger may be just a word, but if I do the things that define anger, anger is then no longer just a word, because I have given to it spirit and life. **This is how many spirits enter:** through words and acting on those words.

If someone says they will kill, then the spirit of murder is of none effect until murder is done through action. Though it is illegal for spirits to enter into this realm without a physical body, they may gain access through, or because of our words.

It is words that identify us as being created into the image of God. Everything that was created was created, after God had spoken it into existence. Likewise, the words we speak will either summon the holy angels, (Dan. 10:12) or fallen angels, [demon spirits].

But God has given the believer the Holy Spirit who enables us to become God-inside minded, so that we can know His word, and say what he says. Even when we pray, we should pray God's word back to his by faith, because God promised to honor his own word.

DRAWING SPIRITS

I have noticed, if I talk about something from the past, the spirit of it soon comes into the present atmosphere. If I talk about something painful that has happened to me, I began to feel it all over again, because the spirit of that painful past is being recalled. When I talk about how angry I was, I can feel that same spirit of anger ushering in, just by talking about it.

On the other hand, when I talk about the things of God, I experience the presence of the Holy Spirit and the holy angels. Just as the spirit of anger is waiting for its voice command, the spirit of blessing is waiting for its voice command.

Therefore, let every cursed thing be bound. Let every blessed thing be loosed and free to minister to us and on our behalf.

Without spirits, sickness would be dead, jealousy would be dead, lies etc., would be dead. <u>Inactive</u>. It is spirit-breath or *inspiration* that gives activity to every active thing. Man is a spirit. He has a soul; he lives in a body.

Example: The activity of jealousy is stirred by a spirit. "And the spirit of *jealousy* comes upon him and he be jealous of his wife, and she be defiled: or if the spirit of jealousy come upon him, and he be jealous of his wife, and she be not defiled". (Numbers 5:14)

Hear what the Spirit of Lies says to God:

> And the Lord said unto him, "Wherewith?" And he said, "I will go forth, and I will be a <u>lying spirit</u> in the mouth of all his prophets." And He said, "Thou shall persuade him, and prevail also: go forth, and do so." (1 Kings 22: 20-22)

> And, behold, there was a woman which had a <u>spirit of infirmity</u> eighteen years, and was

> bowed together, and could in no wise lift up
> herself. (Luke 13:11) (In this case sickness is
> a spirit.)

See! Lies are spirit-breathed, lust of the flesh, bitterness, and un-forgiveness. All manner of sin has to have a spirit. But so does love, forgiveness, truth, peace, and all righteousness. Howbeit, there is only one <u>Holy Spirit</u>, and He is of God and God only.

The more we give of ourselves to God and the things of God, the more we rest and live in peace without those unwanted entities.

> And I heard a loud voice saying in heaven,
> 'Now is come salvation, and strength, and the
> kingdom of our God, and the power of His
> Christ: for the <u>accuser</u> of our brethren is cast
> down, which <u>accused</u> them before our God
> day and night.' (Revelation 12:10)

How about that?! One of the many titles for Satan is the *accuser*. He is not only against us, but he has access to God and is able to accuse you and me before God.

The same one who seduces us manipulates and tempts us into doing things his way, then, goes to our heavenly father and says, "Look what your Christian child, your little saint, did".

Satan knows that God loves us so much, that he gave his only begotten son, Jesus, to die for our sins that we may have eternal life after receiving him. The only way he (satan) can get to God is through us.

Therefore, he constantly tries to put his hooks in us, then mocks God by saying, "Look what they did". The sad part is that the devil is almost always right about us, and doesn't have to lie on us because the things which he accuses us of are the kind of things that we call *common* and *natural*.

Well, my friends, as common as we may think those entities are, they still are against God and His will for us. We say un-forgiveness is common or "natural", but God says forgive, because un-forgiveness is against us.

The things which we have surrendered to, or have learned to live with, because we may think we can't help ourselves, we call common or natural. An adulterer gets used to adultery, and then thinks it's natural or common when it seems he can't stop.

Fear, lying, worrying, grief, gambling, drunkenness, fornication, stealing, bitterness, strife, jealousy, backbiting, confusion, and all the many things that break the believer's peace are not common. They are ungodly/unclean spirits.

This is why we must be born again, so that the Spirit of God can indwell us and help us to obey God. Without me you can do nothing, says the Lord. "I am the vine, you are the branches, he that abides in me, and I in him, the same brings forth much fruit: or without me you can do nothing." (John 15:5). Yes, we cannot enter, nor see the kingdom of God's principals without the new birth. (John 3: 3,5).

God said, "As many as I love, I rebuke and chasten". But guess what? God is love, and punishment is not in him. Therefore, the accuser gets to be a part of our discipline. The accuser in Rev. 12:10, that is.

What God does is set the standard, the time, the place, and the limit to what the accuser is allowed to do. Example: "When the enemy shall come in like a flood, the Spirit of the Lord shall lift up a standard against him". (Isaiah 59:19b)

Satan is totally reprobate; he is out of control; his nature is destruction. If God did not set a standard for satan, there would be nothing left of whatever he is allowed to do. But satan can do nothing without God's permission. **Good!** God shows a standard being set in the case of Job. "And the Lord said unto Satan, 'Behold, he is in thine hand; but save his life.'" (Job 2:6)

Revelation knowledge says Satan goes to God and accuses us, the children of God. Then God asks, "What's in it for you? What do you want from them? What is the reason you're accusing them?" After Satan tells Him, if being right in his accusations, then, God sets a standard.

In the story of Job, satan told God what he wanted to do to Job. But God also knew that satan would have killed Job unless He told him not to. (Job 2:6) Satan didn't know exactly what to accuse Job of because the hedge had blocked his view. Job later satisfied the devil's suspicions in Job 3:25, when Job himself said, "For the thing which I greatly feared is come upon me, and that which I was afraid of is come unto me".

Satan had been suspicious that being afraid of losing what he had, was part of Job's faithfulness. But he couldn't prove it because Job's spiritual life was hidden, just as ours (born-again believers) are according to Colossians 3:3, KJV, which says, "For ye are dead [to sin] and your life is hid <u>with Christ</u> in God".

*How easy would communication be without spirits, or inspiration? I imagine it would not be easy at all.

SPIRITUAL ATTRACTION IN TYPE

Two strangers, male and female, are in the presence of one another for the first time ever. They each notice something rather relative about the other. They seek opportunity for a chance to talk. Eventually, they do.

One says to the other, "There's something about you that I like, though I don't know what it is". "I was thinking the same thing about you," replied the other. After talking for a while, they discovered they were at that location for the same reason. They were both lonely and seeking companionship with the opposite sex. We may call it coincidental. But in type, kindred spirits attract one another.

SPIRITUAL CONFLICT

Two males had a very harsh dislike for one another at first sight. They found themselves communicating with one another through third parties. Eventually, the third parties identified the problem and reason for the conflict and learned that,

Both men were proud and boastful, selfish in their thinking, never intending to be outdone. Their spirits knew each other, which caused contention in the men emotions and mental views.

At a young age, I noticed spiritual conflict as an elementary school student, when a tough school bully's girlfriends were always attracted to me.

Why do we love some people at first sight, knowing nothing about them? Why do we sometimes have a harsh dislike for people we have never met? It is because of kindred spirits that are in association or conflict with one another. Our actions are spiritually motivated. Therefore, we might train ourselves to come to a greater awareness that they are present with us each day. And become more observing of human behavior, including that of our own.

Instinctively, I knew that a spirit was trying to draw me into a fight with that bully. If I had thought that I could beat him, then, maybe that spirit would have won me over. But I won; I stayed away from his girlfriends. And avoided a good whipping...

There is a way that we can have all things in common, though it may get rocky from time to time, because we're not perfect. The bible tells us how. Being born again, with each having a heart to please God, we then come as close as possible to acquiring perfect fellowship with one another as illustrated in Acts 3: 44-47:

> "And all that believed were together, and had all things common. And sold their possessions and goods, and parted them to all men, as every man had need. And they continuing daily with one accord in the temple, and breaking bread from house to house, did eat their meat with gladness, and <u>singleness of heart</u>. Praising God, and having

favor with all the people, and the Lord added
to the church daily such as should be saved".

Described above is spiritual attraction. It has been commonly called by many <u>good vibes</u> and <u>body chemistry</u>. But without spirits or inspirations (which are virtually the same) the body would have no chemistry or vibes. It would be just as Adam was before God inspired him with breath.

The Hebrew word for breath is inspiration. Whatever we do is inspired by a spirit--either the Holy Spirit or one of those other spirits. In order for us to be born again, baptized, sealed, indwelt, and led by the Holy Spirit, we must yield our life to Christ and His cause and purpose in the world, then, become the children of God.

Some say everybody is a child of God! Well, in ownership, that's true. But a true child of God belongs to God in fellowship as well, which is done only through the saving grace of our Lord and Savior, Jesus Christ, who Himself said, "No man can come to the Father except by Me".

God cannot lie. Therefore, if lying should play a role in a particular purpose of God, He would have to use a lying spirit to do it. A lying spirit is of Satan. Therefore, God uses the devil. Hear what the spirit of lies says; "I will go forth, and I will be a lying spirit in the mouth of all his, [King Ahab's], prophets". (1 Kings 22: 22)

The Old Testament indicates, but does not explain, how God allowed the production of evil punishment upon men. Therefore, many Bible readers have thought that evil came from God. Actually, it is allowed by God rather than produced by him.

It was always meant for man to acknowledge the full sovereignty of God. God is in control regardless of who is allowed to produce evil or punishment. Whatever is not done according to God's perfect will could be done only by his permissive will. <u>God is judge of all</u>! Satan is a created being and can do nothing unless God permits, set a standard, a time, and place for what he allows, or uses the devil to do.

Years ago, I asked a group of people if they loved God. Each of them replied, "Yes." Then I asked if they hated the devil. To this day, I have not received an answer from any one of them. But once we are born again the answer becomes easy because we can see the difference. It becomes clear that One loves us while the other hates us, and we return to each his own.

As mentioned earlier from Acts 2, the Holy Spirit causes the born-again to have all things in common. But, unclean spirits also manifest common ground of all things in common.

THE PROVINCE OF HINDRANCE

Unclean spirits are hindering spirits in the life of the child of God. They even hinder the praying results of the husband when he doesn't properly honor his wife in Christ through the word.

1 Peter 3: 7 says, "Likewise, you husbands, dwell with them, [the wife], according to knowledge, [godly wisdom] giving honor to the wife, as unto the weaker vessel, and as being heirs together of the grace of life; that your prayers be not hindered".

LOOKING BACK

As mentioned earlier, looking back reminds me how we are invaded, and sometimes bombarded by what the Bible calls 'unclean spirits' at such young ages, sometimes as early in life as before or after we are born.

The spirit of retaliation manifested in me soon after reaching age 12. I can recall the door I opened to let him in. It was the door of a wounded spirit. I felt slighted, ignored, and uncared for. Resentment and Anger were with me as I began to think of a way to get back at them. [I used resentment and anger]. Then, the spirit of retaliation entered.

"There must be some way that I can get back at the person or people that are doing things to make me feel this way", I thought to myself. Therefore I began to steal from them. And, each time I did, something in me--the spirit of hurt that is--was satisfied.

Since spirits don't die, retaliation was only one of the spirits I needed to be *delivered* and set free from after I received the new birth. When I stopped retaliating at about age 15, the spirit of anger and bitterness was still alive and well in me, ready to go with me into the future, and I slept with them for years to come.

One day, while on the high school campus, I noticed some of my classmates looking sad, but not really sad. Actually, they appeared solemn and gloomy. I asked one of them that was standing alone what was wrong with those other kids.

He said, "They're in love!" Well, I didn't know what love was, but I wanted to know what they felt because it seemed whatever they felt was something special but not really painful. So I picked out a pretty girl who happened to be about two years younger than I was but as pretty as one I wouldn't mind falling in love with.

I fell in love with her. But I didn't know that it was the wrong kind of love. It was a love that made me crazily jealous. One that made me violent toward anyone I saw talking to her other than some of my most trusted friends. That kind of love also made me so selfish that I would do almost anything to have her all to myself, including intentionally impregnating her.

One day she told me that she was pregnant. That made me happy, though we were both still in high school. I just wanted her. I prepared myself for a family, thinking, "I know I've got her now; she's going to have a baby. She's stuck with me."

Gladly, I quit school, got a job, and was looking for a place for us to stay, when she told me that she was no longer pregnant. By then, I had no more interest in school. Therefore, I stayed out and pursued a GED diploma, and off to the world I went. But anger, bitterness, and retaliation were still with me.

One of the first things I thought to do was to protect myself from ever falling in love like that again. I never wanted to be hurt and disappointed again. But I loved girls and was, somehow, attracted to many of them. I made it hard for a girl to be just friends with me.

Going from girl to girl, I became one of the world's greatest liars. I loved them all, but not the way I should've, and certainly not the way they wanted me to. In fact, I did it for so long that I thought it was alright with God, as though, it was a calling on my life, or I was God's gift to females.

I never felt convicted, condemned or guilty. Nor did I realize the consequences of sinful deeds done in the body. The spirit of lies was very much alive in me, protecting my self control-driven desires. The lying spirit was able to work well in me because I always spoke more truth than lies. Most of my lies had some truth in them, along with good intentions.

Lying was one of the last spirits that I was delivered from. As I watched him leave me, I was happy to have my wife as a witness. But since she had experienced his work in me for years, it wasn't easy for her to accept the fact that he was gone. Years have since passed. She doesn't seem to suspect the spirit of lies indwelling me anymore.

Did I know then that I had those spirits? No! Did I want to be ruled by unclean, lustful spirits? No! No one does, especially when you know that there is a God--a true, loving God.

Enticing spirits never reveal truth about the real outcome or consequences of the wrong that they seduce us into doing. But the Holy Spirit will teach us the truth of all things, and even show us things to come, according to John 16:13: "Howbeit, [although] when He, the Spirit of truth, is come, He will guide you into all truth: for He shall not speak of Himself; but whatever He shall hear, that shall He speak: and He will show you things to come."

Though the influence of satanic forces may seduce, entice, or tempt us, they still go before God and accuse us, *Day and Night*! (Rev. 12:10). They are definite enemies that rest in us even while we sleep.

IT'S A SETUP!

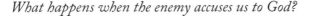

What happens when the enemy accuses us to God?

What happens when we are accused in the court system? The accusation has to be proven to be true. If so, then there is a penalty. *God does not uphold us in our wrong doings.* Therefore, when the accuser accuses us, usually he is right, because he is the one who help us to disobey our God.

The same one who persuades us to sin against God is the one who goes to God and turn us in. He, then, plays a role in our punishment as we read earlier in the case of King Ahab.

THE SPIRIT OF CONFUSION

Never try to match wits with the devil apart from or without the word of God. <u>Tell the devil what is written</u>, as Jesus did according to Luke 4: 3-13). Otherwise, he will confuse us as he did Eve in the garden.

Eve tried to match wits with the enemy, but he confused her. In Genesis 3:3, her confusion was manifested when she added to what God had originally said, with her phrase, *"neither shall you touch it"*. But God had said, "But of the tree of the knowledge of good and evil, thou shall not eat of it."

The word, "gam" {the Hebrew word for "yea"], in Genesis 3:1, *meaning,* [as we were saying, or even though] indicates that this was not the first time the serpent had a conversation with Eve. Genesis 3:6 may indicate the same thing, as Adam was amongst them (as though he was waiting to see what would happen if she ate). That verse says, "She took the fruit thereof, and did eat, and gave also to her husband with her; and he did eat".

Matching wits with the enemy doesn't work. When I was a gambler, each time I made up my mind that I would quit, I would win again. But when I faked it, I continued to lose. That's when I learned that I couldn't psych out the devil; he knew when I meant what I said.

On the very day that I quit smoking marijuana, someone brought a bag of it, and gave it to me, and said, "Its free; it's a gift".

When you have been delivered, Satan will always come back to test you. He will test you with whatever always used to work.

Even at the end of Jesus' temptation, the Bible says, "And when the devil had ended all the temptation, he departed from him for a season." (Luke 4:13) He always come back to try again.

Guess who was talking to Jesus when He said, *"Get thee behind me, Satan."* (Matthew 16:23, AMP) Jesus recognized that it was Satan using Peter's voice to rebuke the will of God. (v.21) Jesus was sharing with his disciples, his future sufferings, death, and resurrection, when Peter decided to rebuke Him. Peter was exalting his own words against the word of God, which 1 Corinthians 10:5 tells us not to *allow*. What a wake-up call that must have been to Peter. (Maybe that would have helped me to watch what I said from that point on.)

"*The devil is a lie!*" is the term many of us use today rather than calling other people the devil. But we do show that we realize that someone other than God is speaking to us, and we are rebuking it. **GO, SAINTS!**

FREEDOM FROM UNCLEAN SPIRITS

AM I EVER FREE FROM THE INFLUENCE OF UNCLEAN SPIRITS?

Yes! But not exempt!! No one since the fall of Adam and Eve has ever been exempt, with the exception of the Lord Jesus Christ, whom God gave the Holy Spirit without measure. "For he whom God has sent speaks the word of God: for God gives not the Spirit by measure unto Him." (John 3:34)

If we could avoid ever being under the influence of such things as anger, envy, hurt, worry, gossip, fear, depression, sorrow, jealousy, lust, gluttony, etc., or any other negative adjectives, then we may prove to be at least, temporarily, spirit free.

The truth is, though we're not exempt, or ever free from those invisible entities," yet, having the Holy Spirit enables us to control them, rather than allowing them to control us.

Casting them out is part of our Christian identity. It's our trademark; it's what we do, according to Mark 16: 17-18. As believers, we must take authority, take our place in Christ, and by faith use the word of God in the name of Jesus as Christ has commanded and has promised that the devil would obey us.

SATAN, I REBUKE YOU!

Recently, I learned that when we say to the devil, we rebuke him, we're not rebuking him at all, and he is probably laughing at us. We can't rebuke the devil by merely saying, "I rebuke you." We have been given authority. We rebuke Satan the same way that Jesus did. Jesus never said, "Satan, I rebuke you." He rebuked him by being authoritative, telling him what to do and what not to do.

When Jesus wanted Satan behind him, he told him to get behind. In Mark 9:25, Jesus rebuked the devil in the following way; "<u>You dumb and death spirit, I charge you, come out of him, and enter no more into him</u>."

So we rebuked the devil by giving him a command according to the word of God in the name of Jesus. We must, first, identify that spirit according to his personality, character, or manifestation. Then take authority in the name of Jesus, and command the spirits to leave whomever our deliverance ministry is ministering to.

Rebuke means belittle, talk down on, etc. Therefore, we can't rebuke the devil until we exercise our authority through the word of God, in the name of Jesus.

Moreover, demons know when we are confident in our faith and whether we mean what we say. This is why God did not give us the spirit of fear. But he did give unto us the spirit of power, of love, and a sound mind. (2 Timothy 1:7)

ACCEPTING THE PERSONALITIES OF OTHER PEOPLE

Having observed the activities of spirits has helped me to understand human behavior better and has blessed me with patience in dealing with various personalities.

Regardless of the behavior of others, even when I say I don't know why they do whatever, I usually quickly come to the conclusion that I do know, and I do understand. They are simply under the influence.

I understand from the standpoint that Jesus was able to look down upon His haters from the cross and say, "Father, forgive them, for they know not what they do."

He knew what was in man: "But Jesus did not commit Himself to them, because He knew <u>all men</u>, and needed not that any should testify of man: for He knew what was <u>in man</u>." (John 2: 24-25)

As born-again believers, we have the same Holy Spirit in us that Jesus had in Him. Jesus said, He [the Holy Spirit] would not only teach us the truth of all things, but would show us things to come. (John 16: 13)

If you don't know a person by their spirit, you probably don't know as much as you could. I know that in the natural sense we usually focus on sights and sounds or the way people look and act, the sound of their words, etc. But it pays huge dividends to know the difference between the Word of God and the words of the world when people are talking. Sound is what tricked Eve; sight, or the way things seemed to be, is what tricked Adam.

These traits are in the natural man's genes today. We were born with them, which is one of the reasons why the Lord has said, 'we must be born again'. We must not only be made fit for heaven, but, also, be made fit for use in the Master's kingdom, here and now.

In saying I now understand varieties of human behavior I mean that I, as did our Lord, know what is <u>in man</u>. Every man!

The real, never-dying us, is our spirit. It is who we are on the inside, the part that can't be seen by the most powerful microscope. Without the human body, you and I would still be alive, but in spirit form only, and incapable of operating in the earth (natural) realm.

No one does anything that others aren't subject to do, or are not capable of doing. It's just a matter of whose spirit we are led by when we do them, whether the devil [<u>world</u>] or the Spirit of God [Holy Spirit].

Identifying different spirits is not hard to do unless we don't know the Word of God. If I am a liar, then I have a lying spirit. If I am gluttonous, I have the spirit of gluttony. Adulterers have the spirit of adultery. According to the Holy Scriptures, spirits are known or identified by their personality and character.

Therefore, when you decide to deliver yourself from those unpleasant, unwanted entities, <u>simply</u> agree with what the Holy Bible says about you and disagree with the thing that you have acknowledged in you that is not of/ from God.

Adhere to James 4: 7: "Submit yourselves, therefore, to God; resist the devil, and he will flee from you." Remember! If we are not honest with ourselves, we're not honest, <u>period</u>. Admitting who we really are, is usually the first step toward deliverance. In the saying of Christ, 'they know not what they do', leads to biblical proof that even Satan didn't know what he was doing.

1 Corinthians 2: 7-8 says, "But we speak the wisdom of God in a mystery, even the hidden wisdom, which God ordained before the world unto our glory; which none of the <u>princes of this world</u> knew: for had they known it, they would not have crucified the Lord of glory."

See there! When Satan induced, urged, and promoted the killing of our Lord, Satan didn't know that he was, at the same time, forfeiting his own kingdom, which he had stolen from Adam and Eve.

The two major parts of God's ultimate plan for man's eternal life are: (1) salvation for the soul of man (2) a final judgment and destruction of Satan.

Satan was created, but evil was not. Evil has always had its own place in existence, but evil can be destroyed only by good. Therefore, God, having all wisdom and power, will righteously judge evil and destroy it once and for all.

Evil, and everything it stands for and everyone included in it, will be, ultimately, destroyed by the second death called, Hell. A permanent separation from God and everything God stands for.

THE GREAT WHITE THRONE JUDGMENT

And I saw the dead, small and great, stand before God; and the books were opened: and another book was opened which is the book of life: and the dead were judged out of those things which were written in the book, according to their works.

And the sea gave up the dead which were in it; and death and hell delivered up the dead which were in them: and they were judged every man according their works.

And death and hell were cast into the lake of fire, this is the second death. And whosoever was not found written in the book of life was cast into the lake of fire.

(Revelation 20: 12-15; 20:10 and 14: 9-11)

Life for spirits on earth began with man and will end with man. Without physical man, there would be no spiritual life on earth, because a physical body is essential for <u>any</u> spirit to dwell in earth's realm.

Christians, we have a job to do. We are the body of Christ. The Bible declares that Jesus is the head of all things to the church. (Eph. 5:23)

Therefore, we must rid ourselves of ungodly spirits for more reasons than one. (1) We must stop them from hindering us from having, doing and being, all that God has intended for us in this lifetime. (2) We must allow God to clean us up for His return, whether via natural death or rapture.

> Husbands love your wives, even as Christ also loved the church, and gave Himself for it; that He might sanctify and <u>cleanse</u> it with the washing of water by the word. That He might present it to Himself a glorious church, not having spot or wrinkle, or any such thing; but that it should be holy, [separated], and without blemish, [the harboring of ungodly spirits]. (Ephesians 5: 25-27)

WILL POWER

A spirit-possessed person may possibly account for having his will dominated by spirits but most people are not possessed by demons. Most of us, whether saved or unsaved, are still in control of our will and free moral agency.

We are allowed by Almighty God, to imagine, think, believe, and do whatever we will, including breaking laws. Consequences or rewards are our choice. Therefore, spirits can only offer temptations and suggestions. Choosing to agree or not to agree with them is done by us.

Though it benefits them [spirits] greatly when we take the credit for all the thinking and planning is done by us, we are willing to grab the credit when things seem to turn out good, and look for someone else to blame when it doesn't. We usually don't blame the right source, which is the influence of spiritual activities. Instead, we blame other people.

No one is ever, actually, forced to do anything against their will. If it seems so, they are merely surrendering their will to a given situation or thing. Yet, we may say, "They made me do it." Therefore, ridding ourselves of unclean spirits is done by choice, our choice.

As Christians, we choose to be more like Christ, to be sanctified, walking in obedience to the word of God, to the best of our abilities with the help of God. When we do this, He will meet us there.

The keys to the door of not sleeping with the enemy are: (1) believing the fore-mentioned entities do indwell us; (2) being honest with ourselves: things we do apart from God's word, is not of God; (3) identify the spirits by their nature; (4) turn against them and move toward God.

James 4:7 says they will flee from us, leaving them homeless and without a body. Dominate and intimidate them by praising God no matter what, by loving others no matter what and demonic presences won't be able to stand you. "And He said unto him, 'Come out of the <u>man</u>, you <u>unclean</u> spirit." (Mark 5:8)

Jesus paid attention to words. When we know the Word of God, we are able to identify the words that are not of God. When we do, then we know that it's a different spirit.

"And He called unto Him the twelve, and began to send them forth two by two; and gave them <u>power</u> over <u>unclean</u> spirits." (Mark 6:7) The power Jesus gave to His disciples is no less than the power He has given us today, as born-again believers. The power is given to believers, and unless we believe, we cannot prove that we are, who we say we are, because signs will follow, according to Mark 16: 16,17.

When we are not walking by faith, in confidence, with boldness in the Holy Spirit, and firm in our belief, then the spirits will not respect and obey us. They know we are not sure of whom we are.

The spirit of scriptural error was always prevalent in the church. But, today, spirit of compromise taking the lead, or, has become a leading spirit. He is trying to get us away from sound doctrine and into reasoning. And, into what makes sense in the natural, or just sound true.

Unclean spirits use our reservations against us. When we are ready to take a stand for what we know is truth and right, they condemn our conscience with things about ourselves that we know aren't right; thereby, demising our spirit of boldness, and causing us to compromise truth.

THE HOLY SPIRIT: *OURS FOR THE ASKING*

"How much more shall your heavenly Father give the Holy Spirit to them that ask Him?" (Luke 11:13) The Holy Spirit is the only spirit that will lead us into the way of the Lord. If we don't have the Holy Spirit, just ask your heavenly Father, and He will help us in our efforts to stop sleeping with the enemy.

"Goodbye, spirit of un-forgiveness! Spirit of lust, I command you in the name of Jesus, leave me now and never return! My body is the temple of the Holy Ghost. Leave me, anger, lies, depression, stress, gluttony, worry. I intend to expose every one of you, and repent, [turn away from]."

LIVING WHILE UNDER THE INFLUENCE

Many drivers have been ticketed for driving while under the influence of something. Before we are born of the Holy Spirit of God, without realizing it, I believe we, in some ways, pay an unnecessary price for living under the influence of invisible entities, [ungodly spirits].

With the presence of the indwelling Holy Spirit, we can and shall be free from the practice of harboring God's enemies and ours. The new birth gives us that ability. Ephesians 4:27(b) says, "neither give place to the devil." Jesus said this, "Hereafter I will not talk much to you: for the prince of this world cometh, and has nothing, _no place!_ in me." (John 14:30)

SPIRITS DON'T SLEEP

Spirits don't sleep. Therefore, it is actually their nature that we sleep with. Man is a spirit [God breathed]. (Genesis 2:7) He lives in a physical body, [the part that goes back to dust], and he has a soul, [mind, will, emotion]. Therefore, without the human body, neither should need sleep.

How do I sleep with the enemy? I sleep with the enemy by giving him place in me, doing some of the following: if I should steal, worry, fear, pride, lust, envy, or any of the almost innumerable things that are not of God, and harbor them (not exposing, confessing or repenting).

When I sleep, they are still dwelling in me, in my soul (whether mind, will, or emotions). They are alive in me, causing problems in my physical body, binding and hindering me from many of my potential blessings and calling.

Unclean spirits even hinder prayers in marriages, when we husbands forget that we are heirs together of the grace of life.

I recall that after I kicked out lies and other spirits, _blame_ was one of the last to go, with the help of the Lord.

These things can't be done without the help of the Holy Spirit. The Holy Spirit revealed and exposed the spirit of blame. Then God commanded me to never again blame my wife for anything. That spirit is gone from me. I may have to resist the temptation of blame, but I no longer have to fight a spirit that used to indwell me.

I can't forget how the spirit of lies tried to choke me each time I chose truth over lying. Before I committed myself to being truthful, they never tried to choke me. It was after I made up my mind that I wanted to be free from lying that I began to choke and gag at the very attempt to tell the truth, when asked.

They never choked me about telling outright truth, but if it was truth about something I had previously lied about, I would choke and lump up in the throat. Then I began to understand what was happening whenever I felt that way. It was the spirits that were putting up a resistance to come out. But, as I persevered, I was finally free from the spirit of lies.

The spirit of lies could not return, (having a made-up mind to not lie again), because all fear is gone. Therefore, if you should tell a lie, ask yourself, "What do you fear?" When we lie, it's not for what we want; it's for what we are afraid we can't have.

ALL THE SPIRITS ARE SNEAKY

The sneaky spirit of <u>selfishness</u> was revealed when I was badly sick, after being diagnosed with congestive heart failure. I knew I had faith for my healing. My faith was built on having seen divine healing in my body so many times before.

While I was delaying visits to a doctor, I was saying, "God, heal me as you have always done". I prayed that over and over, as time went by. Meanwhile, my wife, relatives and friends were praying for both my healing and that I would show common sense enough to go to a doctor.

By the time my body had accumulated about fifty two pounds of fluid, and I was saying, "Lord, if this sickness is unto death, thank you for saving my soul, I gave my life to you. Therefore, I'm ready to die."

Then the Lord said to me, "*You are selfish*! You are not thinking about your wife, her prayers, her love for you, or how she would fare without you. You haven't even prayed for anything you would like to live for."

Well! If you have never been rebuked or chastised by God, you can't imagine how words like that, coming from a loving, all-knowing God, can make you feel. Briefly putting it, the spirit of selfishness left me that day and he knows not to come back.

Man became a spirit being, as well as spiritual, after God breathed into his nostrils the breath of life. (Genesis 2:7) The Hebrew word for breath is, *N' shamah*, [nesh-aw-maw], meaning "wind, soul, spirit, inspiration."

In creation, man was seen as inactive without a spirit. Before the fall, God gave Adam the spirit of man, also called the spirit of the flesh. Satan, via manipulation, stole everything that God had given man except his body, when he robbed him of the kingdom called Eden.

God did not indwell man throughout Old Testament times. But the Spirit of God would come upon man to empower him for special purposes. [Moses, Samuel, David, the prophets, etc.]

Today, man is led by one of two spirits: The spirit of God or the spirit of Satan. (Sometimes both, especially if he is a carnal man) [read Romans 7:15-21] As written in Frank and Ida Mae Hammond's book, *"Pigs in the Parlor,"* our bodies, the temple of the Holy Ghost, are God's parlor. Therefore, we must get those pigs [unclean spirits] out of our parlor.

Jesus instructed and gave us the authority to **cast** (toss, throw out) those unclean spirits, saying it would be a sign of our identification with him, if we believe. "And these signs shall follow them that believe; in my name shall they cast (toss, throw-out) out devils." (Mark 16: 17a)

Thank God for the Holy Ghost! For it is He who shed light, expose, and reveal the difference between the godly and the ungodly to us. Although our failing to heed can become a habit of ignorance and continued imprisonment, it's never God's fault.

SPEAK TO YOUR MOUNTAIN (Mk. 11:23)

I thank you Heavenly Father, that you did not give me the spirit of fear, but the spirit of power, of love, and a sound mind. <u>Therefore</u>, *spirit of fear, I'm talking to you right now. Jesus said you would obey me. I willfully turn against you, I renounce your presence in me, I command you to leave my being. Now! In the name of Jesus, according to the Word of God, I resist you, and command you to **flee** from me.* (James 4:7)

True confession is, both, admitting to God and turning our back on sinful acts. (1John 1:9) In the above passage of scripture, God promises to, both forgive me of my sins and cleanse me, which is why admitting is not enough. I have often confessed (admitted) specific sins to God, without any intentions of quitting the doing of the thing.

Maybe God was forgiving me each time I confessed, but because He knows everything, He knew that I would keep confessing and keep going back to the same sins. This mean I had never truly repented. Repent means to [turn from], not merely being sorrowful as many may choose to believe.

I have been sorrowful and cried many tears. But that didn't stop me from going back, over and over again, continuing in my sinful acts.

If anyone <u>could</u> fool God, I would have been one of them.

The first temptation in the Garden of Eden was not one of hunger nor the attraction of beauty but the revelation that man's imagination (Gen. 6:5) has in its nature, a spirit that makes him want to be independent of God. This is why we usually have to prove to ourselves that we need God, before we ever turn to him for salvation.

In studying the three factors that many bible commentators describe as man's failure in the Garden of Eden: (1) the eyes (2) the ears (3) the pride of life, neither was described by God in Genesis chapter six. He [God], imposed it all on man's imagination, although man's imagination is a gift from God. (Gen. 6:5)

In this passage, God said man's imagination is vain from his youth. Well, Adam was never a boy in creation but, spiritually, he was in the infancy of his existence.

It was Adam and Eve's imagination that the enemy worked on in tempting them with the forbidden fruit. The more they imagined the fruit not being harmful, the better it began to look to them. Then, they ate of it.

From that moment, future generations were born with what God has called "vain imagination". It has a spirit of independence which is an inclination to be independent of God. This is why Adam ran <u>from</u> God rather than <u>to</u> God, when God called his name.

One of the hardest things that the natural man has ever done is put God first, although that would actually be putting God in His rightful place. Even among born-again believers, having the indwelling spirit of God, it's not easy for the believer to put him first.

Everything has a name. Spirits have names, but the name, JESUS is above every name! "Wherefore God also has highly exalted him, and given him a name which is above every name." (Phil. 2:9)

Tumor is a name; cancer is a name. Spirits have names. The spirit of jealousy; his name is jealous. The spirit of fear; his name is fear. We, the saints of God, exalt the name Jesus above everything we know that is not of God.

"What shall we say then to these things? If God be for us, who can be against us?" (Rom. 8:31) Is it God's will for us to be sick? Jesus healed the sick. Is it God's will for us to harbor demonic spirits? Jesus cast them out and gave us authority to do the same.

When Jesus calmed the storm, saying, "Peace be still," was that storm God's will? *Jesus never did anything against the Father's will, for he was perfect in obedience to God.*

We cannot know God's will apart from His word. His word is His will, His will is His word. God, His word and His will are one. Therefore, to know what is not of God and what is not in His will for us, we must come into knowing His Word.

When we are facing adversities, we can properly identify our adversaries, and say to them, *"This situation doesn't line up with the Word of God for my life and it has to go,* in the name of Jesus!

KEEP THE FAITH AND KEEP IT SIMPLE

Many of us do sleep with the enemy and many of us have slept with the enemy. Those of us who have, but have learned the power of deliverance, may also know how to be God-inside-minded. We pay attention to the Spirit of God inside us. He reveals everything in us that is not like God. We have learned to act fast in doing what is necessary to rid ourselves of unrighteousness.

Those who ignore the Holy Spirit's warnings will continue to harbor the invisible entities that call our bodies their house and bind/hinder the things that God has called us to be, to have, and to do in the kingdom of light.

We must allow the Holy Spirit, the Word of God, and the name of Jesus, to help us put on the whole armor of God, that we may be able to stand against the struggles and tricks of the evil one. (Eph. 6:11)

In the Holy Scriptures, satanic or demonic spirits are also called devils or unclean spirits. They are seen in Scriptures as speaking through humans, speaking to humans, possessing humans, causing physical and mental illness, accusing God to man, and man to God.

It is believed that though they may occupy a place in the professing believer, they cannot possess a born-again believer, because of the presence of the indwelling Holy Spirit.

Mark 1:23 says, "And there was in their synagogue a man with an unclean spirit; and he cried out". HE cried out (v.24) saying, "Let <u>us</u> alone; what have we to do with you, Jesus of Nazareth. Have you come to destroy us? I know who you are, the Holy One of God. (v.25) and Jesus rebuked him, saying, Hold thy peace, and come out of him."

These verses show that (1) the spirits in that man knew who Jesus was, and (2) that they misinterpreted His purpose and timing. They knew their doom <u>ultimately</u>, and thought Jesus had come to torment them before time.

But Jesus demonstrated portions of His purpose by rebuking the spirits and casting them out of the man.

There is no indication how many spirits were present in the man, but enough for the man to speak the plural phrase, "Have you come to destroy us." (v.26) shows that the demonic spirit was angry for having to leave a human body which had housed him. He caused some type of visible damage and gave an outcry on his way out.

WHERE DID THE UNCLEAN SPIRIT GO?

> When the unclean spirit is gone out of a man, he walks through dry places, seeking rest, and finds none. Then he says, I will return into my house, [the man's body], from where I came out; and when he is come, he finds it empty, swept, and garnished. Then goes he, and take with himself seven other spirits more wicked than himself, and they enter in and dwell there: and the last state of that man is worse than the first. (Mt. 12: 43-45)

Deuteronomy chapter 28 is big on its descriptions of blessings and curses. Both, the blessings and the curses, are real. But God advises the people of God to choose the blessings--choose to do the thing that brings the blessing.

Proverbs 26:2 says, "The curse causeless shall not come". In other words, a curse does not come without a cause. The Good News translation says, "Curses cannot hurt you unless you deserve them."

Unclean, ungodly, unrighteous, demonic spirits are all the same. They are cursed, and they produce after their kind; they produce curses. Sickness is a curse, not a blessing. A lie isn't a blessing. Adultery, fornication, same sex indulging are not blessed things. But it is understandable for those who think so because people have a right to think whatever they choose.

In spite of all the law of God, He still made us free moral agents with a will of our own; which also is why there is a heaven and a hell. We won't go to either place by mistake. We are not here by mistake. Know it or not, we are here on purpose, for purpose. *God has a plan and you're in it.*

DON'T LET 'EM GET AWAY

The sneaky invading entities have been slipping by, while the body of Christ is still trying to discover two-thousand-year-old blessings. We call them kingdom blessings. Many local assemblies in some parts of the U.S. are yet learning about tithing, as though its brand new.

The church has never conquered Hebrews 6: 1-2, [read]. Unfortunately, we are still laying foundations. We seem to think that kingdom living is about nothing more than enjoying financial blessings, at the same time other blessings seem to pass us by. Other than kingdom blessing, there is also, <u>*kingdom authority*</u>.

There is more to kingdom living than what I have in Christ. It is also, who I am, and what I can do, with the authority that's been given to me, with the Word of God, and the name, Jesus!

Many church goers today are complaining about their children's and grandchildren's behavior. Our young people seem unreachable in many ways. We blame it on a variety things, including drugs, alcohol, their friends, hangouts, fatherless, etc. We never seem to consider that the original problems that have plagued man (spirits and spiritual influences) since the Garden of Eden are even more prevalent today.

"Lord, have mercy on my son for he is lunatic, and sore vexed: and, often he fall into the fire, and often into the water." (Mt. 17:15) What did that father say? "Lord, help me with my son, because he is crazy. But it's not his fault." The description we see here is the man's son was plagued with something that manifested itself in a mental and nervous disorder. Something abnormal and unnatural had control of him.

What kind of medicine would be prescribed for him today? What kind of physical medicine can be prescribed to deliver us from demonic forces?

Jesus used the authority given him by God; the authority that has been given to the believer today, according to Mark. 11: 22-24; 16:17-18. He knew that the son's behavior wasn't natural. Therefore, he did not treat it with natural means. Matt. 17: 18 reveals the root of the problem and the cure. Verse18 says, "And Jesus rebuked the devil." Not the fire, not the water. He rebuked the devil. "And, he (the devil) departed out of him: and, the child was cured from that very hour."

I don't know about fighting fire with fire. But I know that the Bible reveals that we must deal with spirits by spiritual means.

> For though we walk after the flesh, we do not
> war after the flesh. For the weapons of our

> warfare are not carnal, but mighty through God to the pulling down of strongholds; casting down imaginations, and every high thing that exalts itself against the knowledge of God, and bringing into captivity every thought to the obedience of Christ. (2 Cor. 10: 3-5)

Often the evil spirits would try to expose who Jesus was before time or too early in His ministry. He would bind them, commanding them not to speak, as in "Hold your peace, and come out of him". (Mk.1:25)

"And he healed many that were sick of diverse diseases, and cast out <u>many</u> devils; and suffered not the devils to speak, <u>*because they knew him*</u>." (Mk. 1:34)

Before the day of Pentecost, when the Holy Spirit was liberally given to all believers, Jesus would temporarily empower His disciples. Mark 6:7 reads, "And he called unto him the twelve, and began to send them forth by two and two; and gave them power over *unclean spirits.*"

God is holy; His spirit is holy; His angels are holy because they remained in the state which He had created them.

The spirit of lies, sickness, disease, depression, grief, and many, many such things are not of God. They contend with the saints and we must contend with them, and enforce the will and plan of God into our lives. This is why He gave us His spirit, His written word, and the name of Jesus.

We don't watch as these unwanted entities take over in our home, in our business, in our children, churches, spouses, etc. (1 Cor. 3: 9) "For we are laborers together with God." Our labor is not in vain in the Lord." (1 Cor. 15: 58)

*They say, you can't stop a bird from flying over your head, but you can stop him from building a nest on it.

BIND THE TREND! STOP THE SPIRITUAL CRISES IN YOU FAMILY.

"And [He] hath made us kings and priests unto God and His Father; to Him be glory and dominion forever and ever. Amen." (Rev. 1:6) Those who believe and practice this portion of Scripture may be trying more and more to enjoy 'the king and kingdom' part, but what about the 'priest' part? The priesthood position in the family is power, authority, and intercessory prayer.

Take authority, take your place in Christ, use His word, His name, by faith, and speak commands against demons and demonic activities in yourself, your spouse, your children, your marriage, your home, and all that God has entrusted to you.

Did you not know that you are a steward and trustee over all that God has given you? "The earth is the Lord's, and the fullness thereof; the world, and they that dwell therein." (Ps. 24:1)

Since everything belongs to God, it makes us only trustees; everything we have and call ours, God has merely entrusted them to us. You have friends because God trusts you with those friends. You have children because He trusts you with them. A spouse, job, money, health and strength, etc. all belong to Him, but He trusts that you will do the right thing.

When I was deep in debt, I was more than happy to learn that my bills belonged to God because when I gave my life to Christ, it included everything. He set me free, but through it all, I learned to be careful with what belongs to Him.

He trusts me with my dependent child, and I refuse to allow demonic spirits to rule him or her. I have the authority in the name of Jesus, to cast demons out of them, out of my house, my spouse, (if she can't help herself and is willing).

> *Remember, He made you king and priest over all that He has entrusted to you; you are responsible and will give account]. (Luke 12: 42-48)*

What a blessed generation we are to be empowered by our Lord and trusted to be laborers together with Him as New Testament saints.

We look at and, sometimes, scorn the younger generation and cultures for the way they do things; even the way they may dress. We despise their pierced tongues, saggy pants, tattoos, etc.

What are they seeking? IDENTITY! They don't know who they are. We must help them by first getting their attention. Then we must teach them who they are, what they have, and what they can do in Christ. The toughest part is to get their attention, then into a mode that will allow us to follow up with our ministry application.

Sadly, we even lose some of them for the lack of the Word in some local assemblies. Many of them complain that they could use more teaching from the pulpits. We must keep praying that church leaders, especially pastors, will get a vision from God concerning the youth.

Young or old, the real battle at hand is spiritual warfare. We must fight the right battle in the right arena. The fight is not flesh and blood. The arena is in the realm of the spirit and the weapons are not physical.

Let us agree with the Word of God and what He says about us. As citizens of the kingdom of God, take from the enemy all that God has said is ours. God's enemy is our enemy. Your enemy is mine, and the same one that is mine is yours.

Let us stop sleeping with the enemy!!!

SIDE EFFECTS AND UNCLEAN SPIRITS (DEMONS)

In the Old Testament, sickness was considered unclean. (Lev. 12: 2) In the New Testament, spirits are considered unclean. (Mt. 10:1; Mk 6:7) Infirmities were associated with sickness. (Luke 13:11) Certain women were healed of both, [evil spirits and infirmities]. (Luke 8:2-3)

We are taught in the Holy Scriptures to use supernatural means to rid ourselves of what we call 'natural sickness', but medical science warns us of the potential side effects which accompany medications which may include even more sickness. So sickness isn't always natural. Therefore, neither might the side effects from medication be natural.

When God heals us, there are no side effects other than those mentioned in Galatians 5:22,23 which says,

"But the fruit of the spirit is love, joy, peace, longsuffering, gentleness, goodness, faith, meekness, and temperance. Against such, there is no law." Wow! That fruit is God's side effects.

I am not saying to stop going to doctors or to stop taking medications. All things are good when done by faith; when not, it is sin. (Rom. 14:28)

ESCAPING THE ENEMY

Five steps in escaping the enemy: (1) identify; (2) acknowledge/ admit; (3) rebuke/renounce; (4) believe/ receive that they are gone; (5) always resist their attempt to return.

1. Identifying demonic spirits is easier when we have learned the Word of Truth [God's Word] and what His Will is for us; to know what is of God and what is not. If it doesn't line-up with what the Word of God says about us, it's not God.
    When they realize that you have identified them, they will sometimes minimize their effects, to make you think they are already gone out.
2. When we acknowledge and admit to ourselves that we carry them, we begin to feel a release, (if we are satisfied with such feeling). We may not have cast them out. The feeling of release is not a trick. It is the Holy Spirit's presence, ready and willing to take over in us, as we continue to surrender to him.

3. When we rebuke them by acknowledging and saying what God says about us, who we are, what we have, and what we can do in Christ, and then renounce them by telling them that we do not accept their unwanted place in us, that we hate them for what they are and have done and *command* them to go in the name of Jesus, **they will leave**!

4. Believe and receive by faith that they are gone. Because Jesus said they would obey you in His name, continue to walk by faith, acting on what you confess to believe.

5. Always resist their attempts to return. Most of the time, when they try to tempt us, they use things that always used to work.

I realized #5 years ago, when I began to notice recurring relationships between male and female; but on the part of females, more than males. Females are usually quicker to return and commit to previous relationships than males, because the same male's lies and pleas still *sound* good. Males might reunite with females that seem easy to get, but they don't usually trust them because they may think that that female is just as easy for other males as well.

I have warned several young females, saying to them, "If you are sexually easy for males they may not trust you afterwards, because they imagine you are just as easy for other males. The tougher and more patient you are will help to win relational trust from most males.

In such situations, in my opinion, it is easier for the enemy to find place to operate in the males; thus, the females fall prey to the inhabiting spirits in the males. Some females have concluded that all males are liars and are no good, for lack of knowing the truth: they slept with the enemy. The invisible influence is not flesh and blood, <u>the Bible warns.</u>

It's not the people; it's the enemy, invisible entities. The Bible tells us that we must forgive people for their faults, but it never tells us that we must forgive <u>spirits</u>.

JESUS KNEW SPIRITS; YOU AND I <u>CAN</u> KNOW THEM

"Beloved, believe not every spirit, but try the <u>spirits</u> [plural], whether they are of God." (1John 4:1a) We have the ability to test them, to examine them. If what they do or say doesn't line up with what God's words says, they are not of God.

WE DO KNOW THEM! We would have to <u>not</u> know right from wrong, to not know them. But usually, we ignore our acknowledgement and awareness. I prove this if I should tell a lie, because I make a decision to lie. I exercise the rights of my free will. There is nothing that stops me from lying; I make a conscious decision whether to tell a lie or the truth.

If I fornicate, no one can force me to fornicate. Twisting my arm or holding me at gun point won't work, if it's against my will. Rape victims may give in to the rapist after being threatened somehow. But many have not given in, even at gun point. Nothing can break our will but God. To all else, we would have to compromise or yield.

Jesus delivered people who were possessed by demons. But, as saints of God, we are not possessed, though they dwell with us. We have enough control with the presence of the Holy Spirit, the written Word of God, and the name, Jesus, to rid ourselves of the forces of darkness that seek to indwell us.

James 4:7, 8a says, "Submit yourselves therefore to God. Resist the devil, and he will <u>flee</u> from you. Draw nigh to God, and He will draw nigh to you."

"You adulterers and adulteresses, did you not know that the friendship of the world is enmity with God? Whosoever therefore will be a friend of the world is the enemy of God." (James 4:4)

SPIRITS KNOW YOU!

"And the evil spirit answered and said, 'Jesus I know, and Paul I know, but who are you?'" <u>In other words</u>, what authority do you have? (Acts 19:13)

In this biblical context, a family which had been practicing exorcism [witchcraft], tried to cast out demons, but was rebuked by them instead. The spirit spoke to them, and said, "I know, recognize, and obey Jesus' and Paul's authority, but who are you?" (Acts 19:15)

You and I should be casting out every identifiable spirit that opposes us, especially in our home, marriage, children, etc., but we must, ourselves, begin to walk in obedience to the word of God. Then we can take our place in Christ, take the authority in the name, Jesus, and rid ourselves and loved ones of the unwanted entities.

The demons, mentioned in Acts 19:15, knew that the sons of Sceva did not have the Holy Spirit nor faith in the Word of God. Neither did they know or practice the Word.

<u>They know you!</u> They know if you are walking by faith in God, they know if you mean what you say when you rebuke them. They know if you believe what you are commanding them to do.

WHEAT AND TARES: THE SATANIC LOOKS LIKE THE REAL THING

2 Cor. 11:14-15 says, "No marvel; for Satan himself is transformed into an angel of light. Therefore, it is no great thing if his ministers, [his spirits, and, people who harbor them], also be transformed as ministers of righteousness; whose end shall be according to their works."

CONCLUSION

Can you think of at least one thing about your ways or your thinking, or your practices that are not like God, of God, or from God? Can you call to mind, thoughts or words in your vocabulary that do not line up with God's Holy Word, (the Bible)? I'm sure we all can. All these are proofs that we not only encounter, but harbor ungodly spirits. These spirits are enemies of, both, God and man. And until our lives line up in agreement with the written Word of God, we are sleeping with these enemies.

They are also called hindering spirits. Jesus said, "They come to kill, steal, and destroy." According to Matthew 18:18, we are supposed to bind them, but when we are not aware of them or don't know our place of authority over them, they end up binding us. According to St. Luke 10:19, Jesus said, "Behold, I give you power to tread on serpents and scorpions, and over all the power of the enemy: and nothing by any means shall hurt you."

Demonic entities fear us as the people of God. They know that if we have knowledge of their presence in us, we would not allow them to tarry. But they rely on the fact that we think that such things as grief, hate, envy, sexual lust, gluttony, depression, etc. are natural, and come through our natural thinking, giving ourselves credit and blame.

In reality, ideas are offered to us by the same means they were offered to Adam and Eve, which is through our very own imagination. Imagination is a gift from God, but when not used in the things of God, God has called the natural man's imagination vain. (Genesis 6:5)

As laborers together with God, we must carry our true identity, according to Mark 16:17, and comply with Matt. 18:18, which is the law of binding and loosing. We should loose ourselves from the bonds of restless spiritual enemies, sending them back into dry desert places where they can find no rest; filling their old place in us with the word of God, applying kingdom principles, for such a time as this.

We are certainly a most blessed generation to be in survival on planet earth in the last days. We may be the generation to witness the glorious rapture of the born-again believers. When we strive to get rid of sleeping with the enemy, we are setting ourselves free for the blessing and power of the Christian harvest.

STEPS TO DELIVERANCE

The first step in my deliverance from indwelling demons was both acknowledging and admitting to myself that I carried them in me. Then I disagreed with their right to dwell in me. I will never forget how 'the spirit of lies' would choke me while on his way out.

In deliverance, the Holy Spirit would recall the lies to me for my confession and repentance. Each time I attempted to tell the truth, something would lump-up in my throat with a fear that would dare me to tell the truth. The Holy Spirit made me aware of what was happening, giving me the courage to press my way through.

Deliverance doesn't come proper without help from the Holy Spirit. The Bible says, 'God is spirit, and they that worship him must worship him in spirit and in truth'. Submitting to deliverance brings one's self into a moment of total truth and surrender to God.

As saints of the harvest, we must work James 4:7, and allow it to work for us, that God may set us free from every evil work.

"Wisdom is the principal thing; therefore get wisdom: and with all thy getting get understanding." (Proverb 4:7)

All Scriptures used in this book are from the King James Version of the Bible, including Scriptural paraphrases, unless otherwise specified.

This book may provide a wealth of information for the person that has or is seeking to come into spiritual warfare, and for the person that seeks to understand, and deal with human behavior from a biblical point of view.

You may learn that Jesus never said, "Satan, I rebuke you." Yet He rebuked him. Understand better the real influence behind human behavior and the risk of self reformation. Spirits don't sleep. How we give spirit to words and why we should say what God's Word says.

ABOUT THE AUTHOR

Frank Young grew up in Ocean Springs, MS, during the mid sixties as a believer in biblical concepts at an early age. Then one day, at age fourteen, while reading his little red Gideon New Testament, he heard a voice saying, "If you keep reading this book, it's going to change your life". For fear of not knowing what was meant by change, Frank closed the book, and did not read another Bible for years to come. Between that time and his appointment to the ordination of church ministry in 1978, Frank lived a very worldly lifestyle while he began a vivid observation of human behavior. Frank is currently an associate minister of the Greater St. Mary Baptist Church in Jonesville, LA.